What Are Literature Pockets?

In *Literature Pockets—Nursery Rhymes* 12 familiar rhymes come alive through fun, exciting projects. The activities for each rhyme are stored in a labeled pocket made from construction paper. (See directions below.) Add the charming cover and fasten the pockets together. Your students now have their own Nursery Rhymes book to treasure.

How to Make the Pockets

1. Use a 12" x 18" (30.5 x 45.5 cm) piece of construction paper for each pocket. Fold up 6" (15 cm) to make a 12"(30.5 cm) square.

2. Staple the right side of the pocket closed.

3. Punch two or three holes in the left side of the pocket.

4. Glue the title strip onto the pocket. The title strip is found on the contents page for each book.

5. Store each completed project in the pocket for that book.

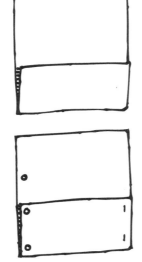

How to Make the Cover

1. Reproduce the cover decoration on page 3 for each student.

2. Students color and cut out the cover and glue it to a 12" (30.5 cm) square piece of construction paper.

3. Punch two or three holes in the left side of the cover.

4. When all the pockets are completed, fasten the cover and the pockets together. You might use string, ribbon, twine, raffia, or metal rings.

Each pocket contains an illustrated copy of a nursery rhyme. Use this chart to introduce or review the rhyme before doing the activities for the rhyme. Here are some suggestions for using these charts:

- Make an overhead transparency of the page. Read the rhyme to students. Talk about the vocabulary and the rhyming words. Point out the words that you would like students to begin to recognize.

- Reproduce a copy for each student to follow along as you read and recite the verse together. Place the copies in the students' individual pockets.

- Mount the page on construction paper and post it on a nursery rhyme bulletin board. When your nursery rhyme study is complete, bind the charts into a cover to create a book for the class library.

Bibliography

Share other nursery rhymes with your students. There are hundreds of nursery rhyme books available in libraries and bookstores. You will find books containing nursery rhymes from around the world as well as classic nursery rhymes. Here is a sampling of the good books you might use.

The Arnold Lobel Book of Mother Goose by Arnold Lobel; Knopf, 1997.

Babushka's Mother Goose by Patricia Polacco; Philomel Books, 1995.

Big Fat Hen by Keith Baker; Voyager Picture Book, 1999.

A Child's Treasury of Nursery Rhymes by Kady MacDonald Denton; Larousse Kingfisher Chambers, 1998.

Chinese Mother Goose Rhymes by Robert Wyndham; Paper Star, 1998.

The Completed Hickory Dickory Dock by Jim Aylesworth; Aladdin Paperbacks, 1994.

Father Gander Nursery Rhymes by Douglas Larche; Advocacy Press, 1986.

Five Little Ducks: An Old Rhyme by Pamela Paparone; North South Books, 1995.

The Glorious Mother Goose by Cooper Edens; Atheneum, 1998.

Grandmother's Nursery Rhymes/Las Nanas De Abuelita by Nelly Palacio Jaramillo; Henry Holt, 1996.

Half a Moon and One Whole Star by Crescent Dragonwagon; Aladdin Paperbacks, 1990.

Hey Diddle Diddle & Other Mother Goose Rhymes illustrated by Tomie dePaola; Paper Star, 1998.

The House That Jack Built by Jeanette Winter; Dial Books for Young Readers, 2000.

If All the Seas Were One Sea by Janina Domanska; Simon & Schuster, 1987.

I Scream, You Scream: A Feast of Food Rhymes by Lillian Morrison; August House Little Folk, 1998.

James Marshall's Mother Goose by James Marshall; Farrar, Straus & Giroux Inc., 1986.

Los Pollitos Dicen/The Baby Chicks Sing by Nancy Abraham Hall and Jill Syverson-Stork; Little, Brown and Company Inc., 1999.

Mary Had a Little Lamb by Sarah Josepha Buell Hale; Orchard Books, 1995.

Mother Goose by Brian Wildsmith; Oxford University Press, 1987.

My Son John by Jim Aylesworth; Owlet, 1997.

Nightfeathers by Sundaira Morninghouse; Open Hand Publishing Inc., 1990.

Nursery Rhymes from Mother Goose: Told in Signed English by Harry Bornstein and Karen L. Saulnier; Gallaudet University Press, 1992.

Off to the Sweet Shores of Africa and Other Talking Drum Rhymes by Uzoamaka Chinyelu Unobagha; Chronicle Books, 2000.

Old Mother Hubbard and Her Wonderful Dog by James Marshall; Sunburst, 1993.

The Real Mother Goose illustrated by Blanche Fisher Wright; Cartwheel Books, 1998.

The Rooster Crows: A Book of American Rhymes and Jingles by Maud Petersham; Aladdin Paperbacks, 1987.

Skip Across the Ocean by Floella Benjamin; Orchard Books, 1995.

Three Little Kittens illustrated by Paul Galdone; Houghton Mifflin Company, 1999.

To Market, To Market by Anne Miranda; Harcourt Brace, 1997.

Tortillitas Para Mama and Other Spanish Rhymes by Margot C. Griego; Henry Holt & Company, Inc., 1987.

Note: Reproduce this cover decoration for students to color, cut out, and glue to the cover of their Nursery Rhymes books.

Name

Pocket Label

A Little Bird

A Little Bird

Once I saw a little bird
Come hop, hop, hop.
And I cried, "Little bird,
Will you stop, stop, stop?"

I was going to the window
To say, "How do you do?"
When he shook his little tail
And away he flew.

© Evan-Moor Corp. • EMC 2700 • Literature Pockets—Nursery Rhymes

1

Once I saw a little bird
Come hop, hop, hop.

A Little Bird

4

When he shook his little tail
And away he flew.

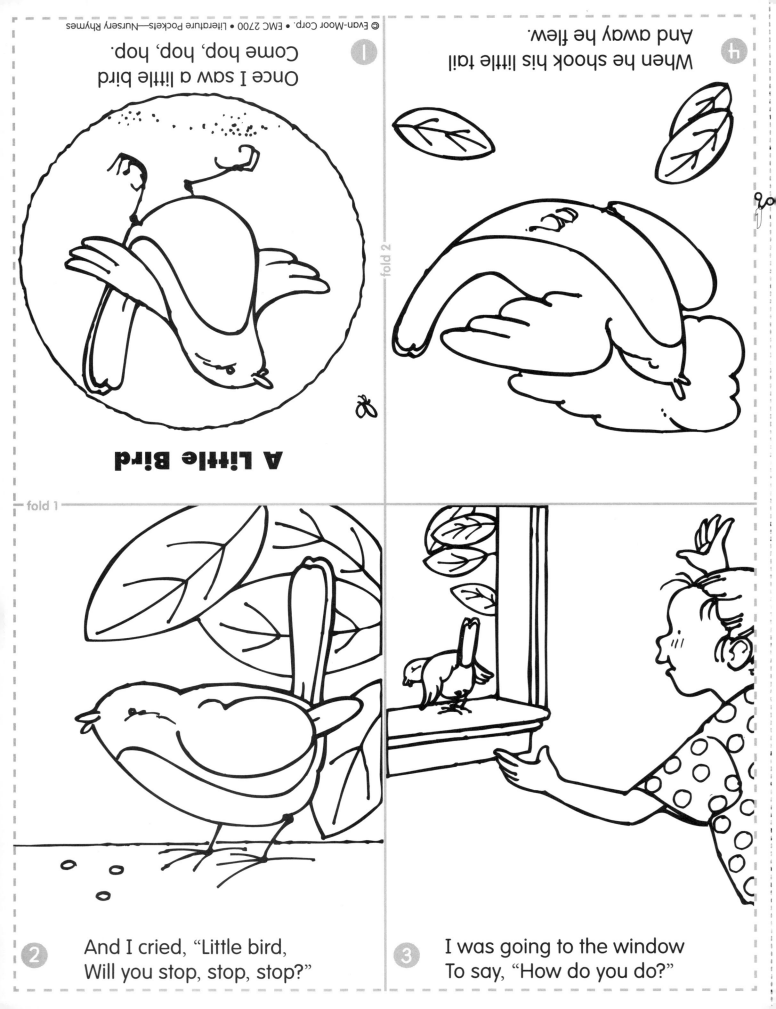

2

And I cried, "Little bird,
Will you stop, stop, stop?"

3

I was going to the window
To say, "How do you do?"

Bird Mitt Puppet

Students use this charming mitt puppet as they recite "A Little Bird."

Materials

- 9″ x 12″ (23 x 30.5 cm) blue construction paper (body)
- 6″ x 9″ (15 x 23 cm) blue construction paper (wings)
- 4″ x 6″ (10 x 15 cm) orange paper (beak and feet)
- templates on page 8
- glue
- black crayon or marking pen

Steps to Follow

1. Follow these steps to make the basic mitt for the puppet.

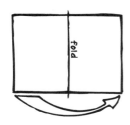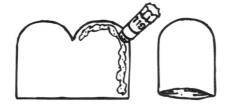

2. Cut out and trace wing templates on the same color construction paper as used for the basic mitt.

3. Cut out and glue the wings to the puppet.

4. Cut out and trace the beak and feet templates on orange paper.

5. Cut out and glue the beak and feet to the puppet. Add black eyes with crayon or marking pen.

6. Slip the puppet on a hand and recite the rhyme for a friend.

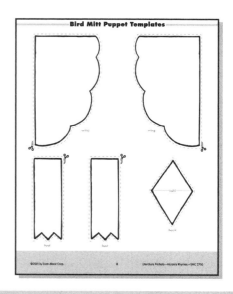

Bird Mitt Puppet Templates

A Little Bird

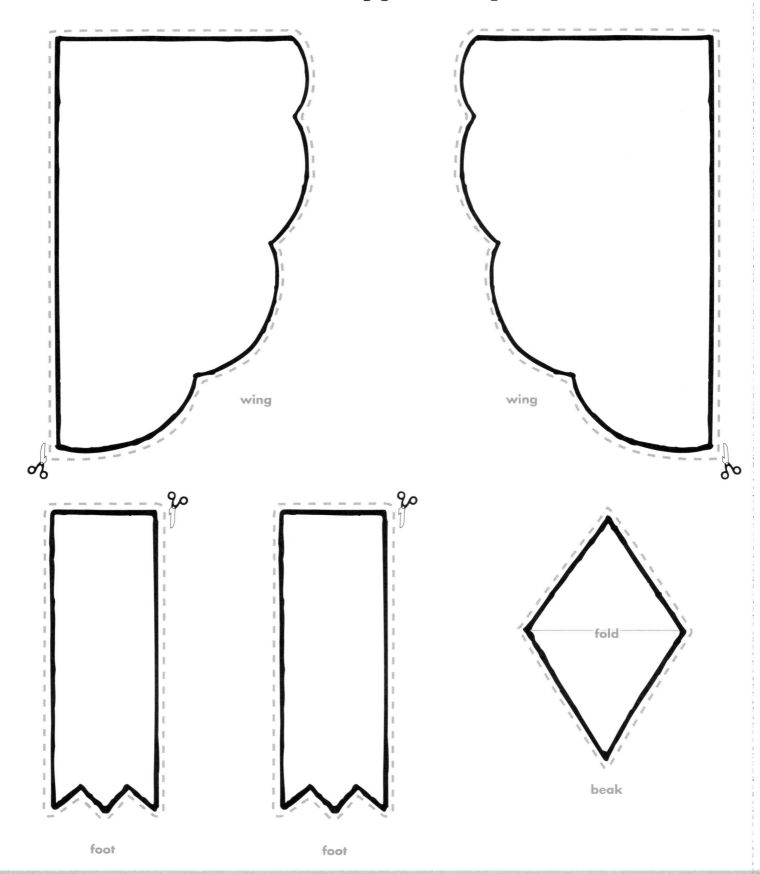

wing

wing

foot

foot

fold

beak

A Little Bird

Literature Pockets—Nursery Rhymes • EMC 2700 • © Evan-Moor Corp.

Name _____

A Little _____

Once I saw a little _____
Come hop, hop, hop.

And I cried, "Little _____,
Will you stop, stop, stop?"

Pocket 2
Little Miss Muffet

Pocket Label

Little Miss Muffet

Little Miss Muffet
Sat on a tuffet,
Eating her curds and whey.
Along came a spider,
That sat down beside her
and frightened Miss Muffet away.

What Is Under Here?
A Flap Book

Students lift the flaps as they recite the nursery rhyme to see what is underneath.

Materials

- 9″ x 12″ (23 x 30.5 cm) assorted colored construction paper
- pages 13 and 14, reproduced for each student
- glue
- crayons
- scissors

Steps to Follow

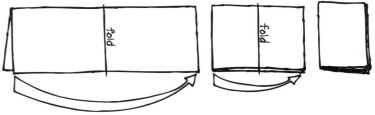

1. Fold the construction paper in half lengthwise, then fold it in fourths as shown.

2. Cut out and glue the poem parts in order on the sections of construction paper as shown.

3. Cut the poem sections apart along the fold lines, stopping at the center of the page.

4. Color and cut out the pictures. Flip each section of the poem open and glue the correct picture under it.

 Little
Miss Muffet
Sat on
a tuffet,

 Eating
her curds
and whey.

 Along came
a spider,
That sat down
beside her

 And
frightened
Miss Muffet
away.

Little Miss Muffet

tuffet

curds and whey

spider

frightened

Literature Pockets—Nursery Rhymes • EMC 2700 • © Evan-Moor Corp.

Things We Sit On

Miss Muffet sat on a tuffet.
Color the tuffet.

Now circle the things you sit on.

Little Miss Muffet

Dangling Spider

1. Color.

2. Cut.

3. Fold.

4. Hang.

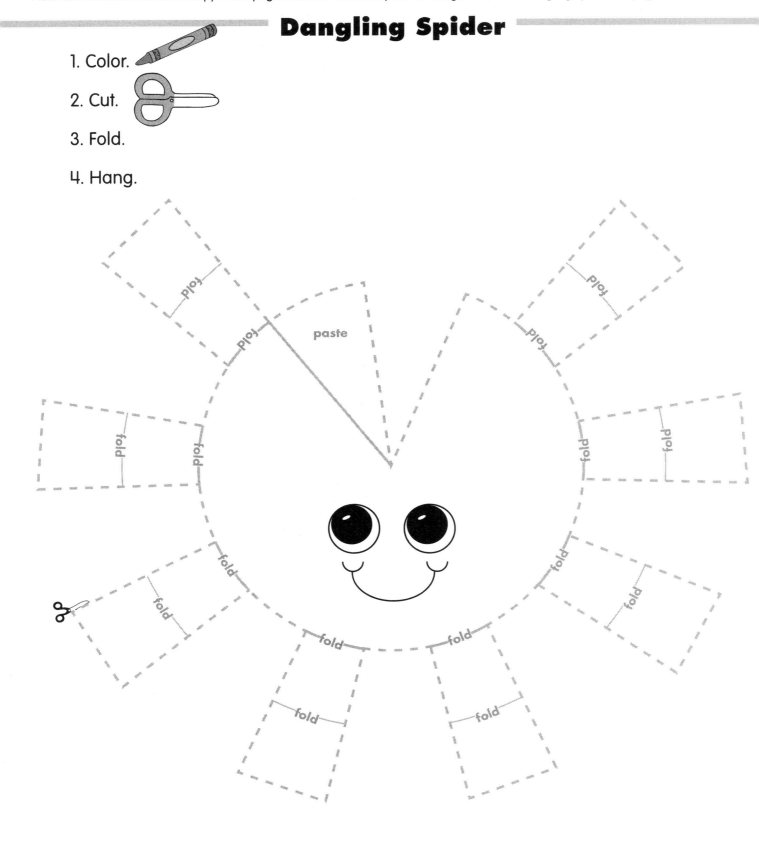

1

name

Spiders

4

Some spiders make webs.

2 There are many kinds of spiders.

3 All spiders have eight legs.

1 2 3 4 5 6 7 8

Pocket 3
My Black Hen

Follow the directions on page 1 for using the nursery rhyme chart.

Just two folds and students have a tiny book of their own to color, read, and then place in their My Black Hen pockets.

Students follow these steps to create a black hen with movable wings. They then work with a partner to recite the nursery rhyme and open the wings to show the eggs Black Hen laid.

Students draw their own hens and then fill in the blanks, giving the color of their hens and naming who the eggs are for.

The first three nests contain eggs for students to count. The last one is empty. Students draw eggs in the nest and write how many they have drawn.

Pocket Label

My Black Hen

My Black Hen

Hickety, pickety, my black hen,
She lays eggs for gentlemen.

Gentlemen come every day
To see what my black hen does lay.

Sometimes nine, and sometimes ten.
Hickety, pickety, my black hen.

1

My Black Hen

4 Sometimes nine, and sometimes ten.
Hickety, pickety, my black hen.

2 Hickety, pickety, my black hen,
She lays eggs for gentlemen.

3 Gentlemen come every day
To see what my black hen does lay.

fold 1

fold 2

Black Hen's Secret

Materials

- pages 22 and 23, reproduced for each student
- 9″ x 12″ (23 x 30.5 cm) black construction paper (body)
- two 6″ x 9″ (15 x 23 cm) pieces of black construction paper (wings)
- scraps of red and orange construction paper (comb and beak)
- white crayon
- 2 paper fasteners per student
- scissors
- glue

Steps to Follow

1. Students cut the hen's body from black construction paper.

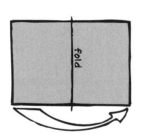

2. Use the templates to cut wings out of black construction paper. Attach the wings to the body with paper fasteners. (An adult may need to poke holes for younger students.)

3. Use the templates to cut out the hen's comb from red paper and her beak from orange paper. Glue the pieces to the hen's head. Add eyes with a white crayon.

4. Cut out and glue the stack of eggs to the hen's body. Move the wings across the body to hide the eggs.

5. Have students work with a partner to recite the nursery rhyme and then open the wings to show the eggs Black Hen laid.

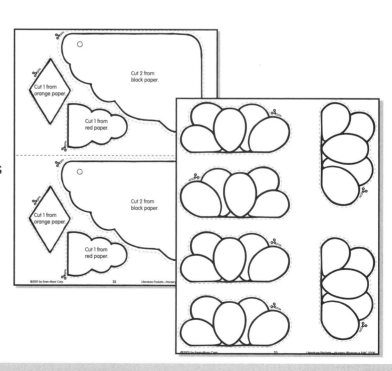

My Black Hen

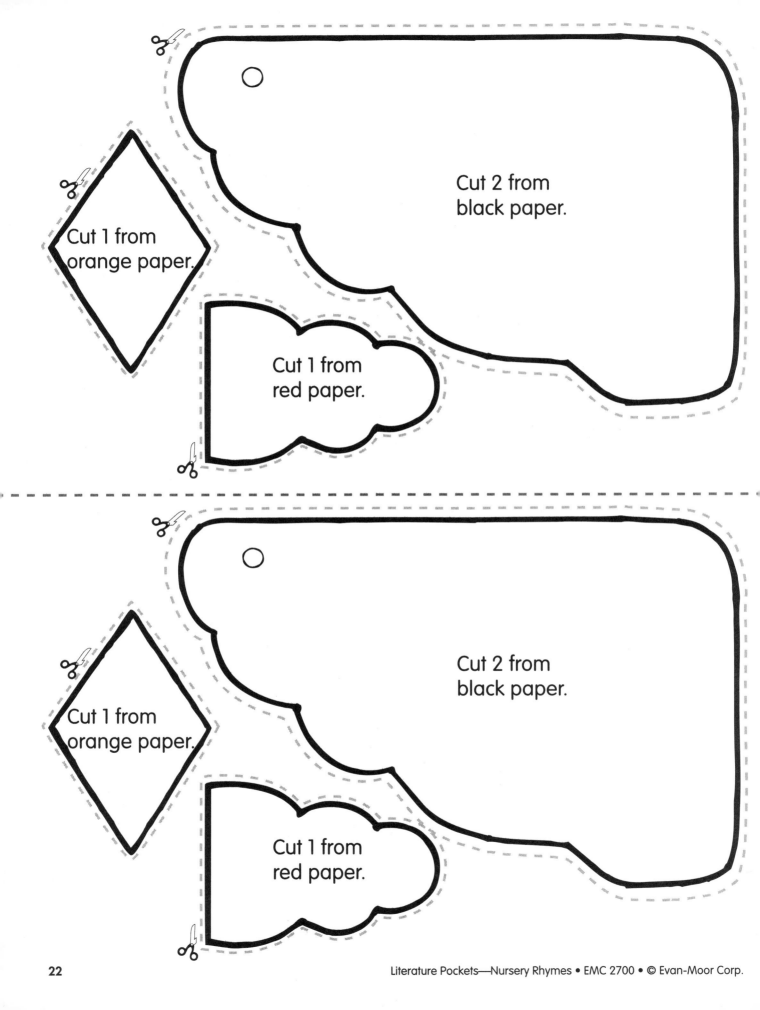

Cut 2 from
black paper.

Cut 1 from
orange paper.

Cut 1 from
red paper.

Cut 2 from
black paper.

Cut 1 from
orange paper.

Cut 1 from
red paper.

 Literature Pockets—Nursery Rhymes • EMC 2700 • © Evan-Moor Corp.

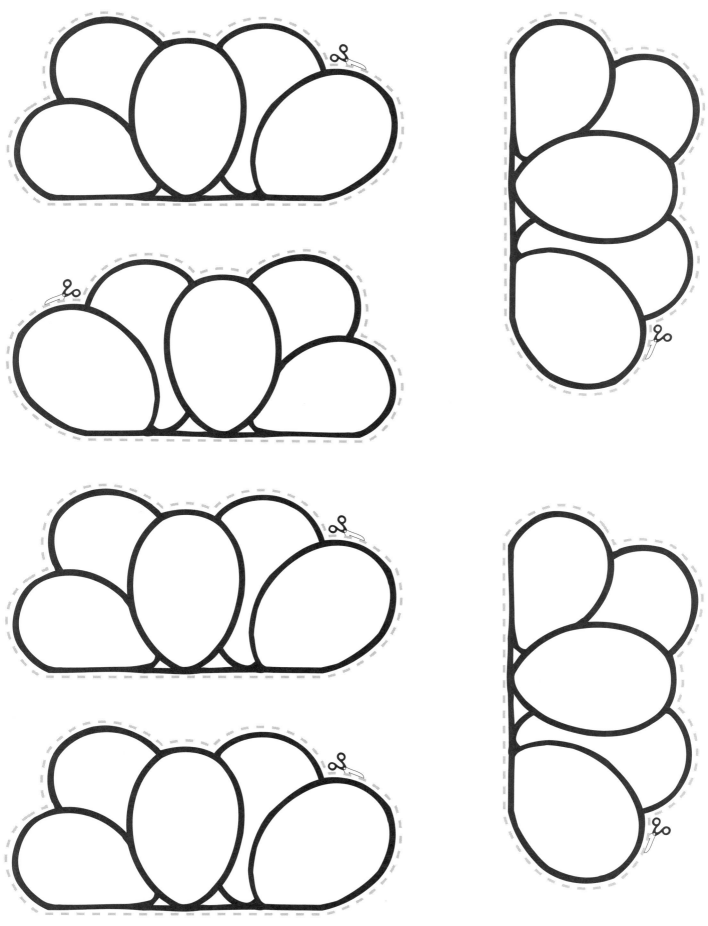

Name _____

_____'s Hen

Hickety, pickety, my _____ hen,

She lays eggs for _____.

Literature Pockets—Nursery Rhymes • EMC 2700 • © Evan-Moor Corp.

Name _____

How Many Eggs Did My Hen Lay?

_____ eggs

_____ eggs

_____ eggs

Draw eggs in the nest.

_____ eggs

Pocket 4
Jack and Jill

Pocket Label

Jack and Jill

Jack and Jill went up the hill
To fetch a pail of water.
Jack fell down and broke his crown
And Jill came tumbling after.

Then up Jack got and off did trot
As fast as he could caper.
He went to bed to mend his head
With vinegar and brown paper.

Name _____

What Happened Next?

Color. Cut out. Paste in order.

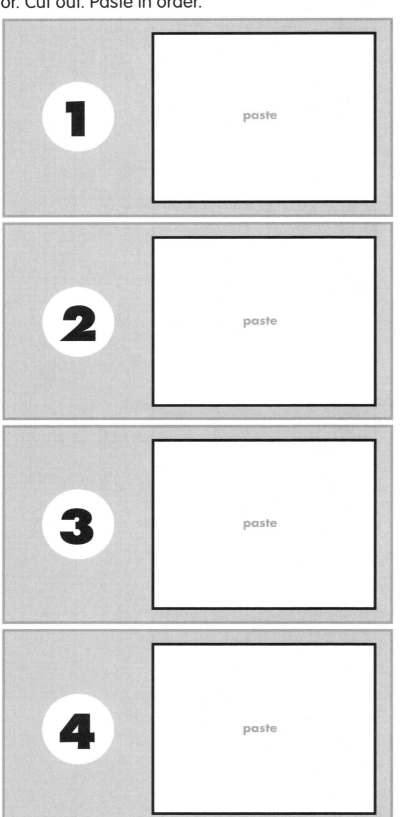

Touch Your Crown

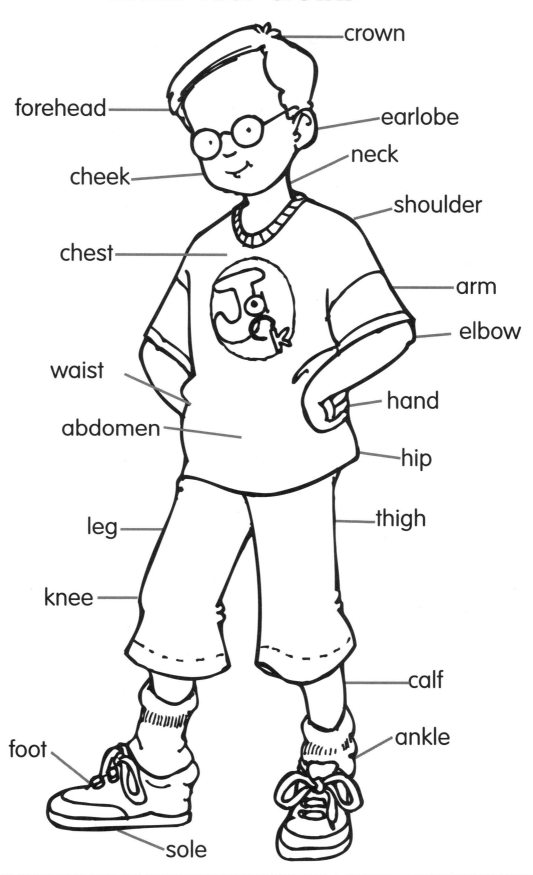

crown

forehead

earlobe

neck

cheek

shoulder

chest

arm

elbow

waist

hand

abdomen

hip

leg

thigh

knee

calf

ankle

foot

sole

Jack and Jill

Jack and Jill Stick Puppets

Name _____

First Aid for Jack

Poor Jack fell down.

Can you help him?

Put bandages where he is hurt.

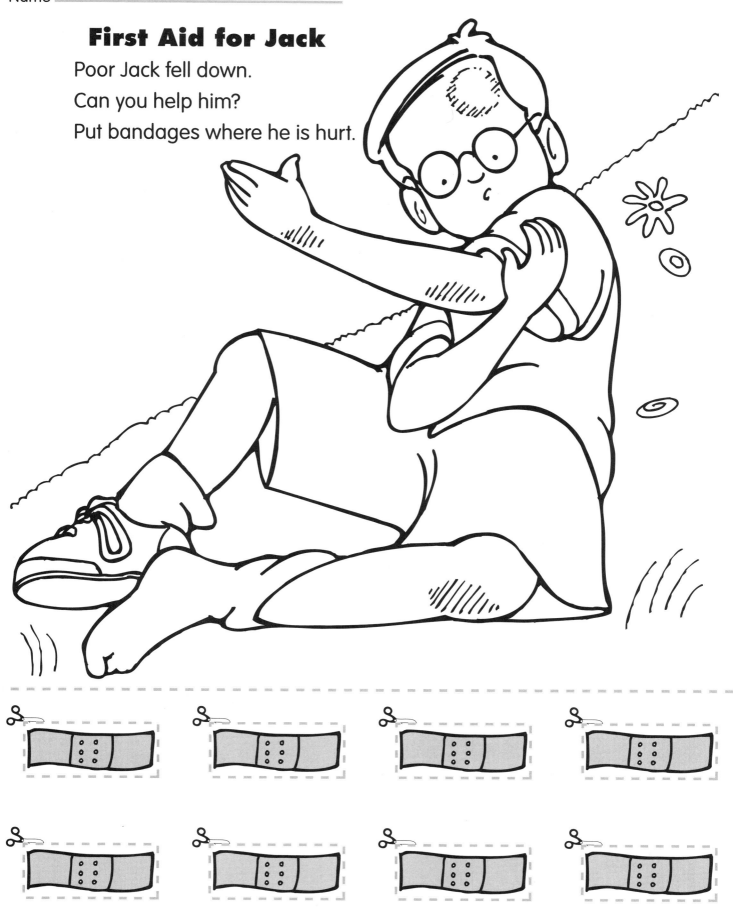

Pocket 5
Little Bo Peep

Follow the directions on page 1 for using the nursery rhyme chart.

This little book will help students remember the rhyme of Bo Peep. As they recite the rhyme, they unfold the pages to see Bo Peep's sheep following after her.

Make fluffy sheep with tails that can wag (with a little help from a friend). This gives students another opportunity to recite "Little Bo Peep."

Bo Peep's lost sheep are hiding in this picture. Students color the sheep, and then count how many they found.

Pocket Label

Little Bo Peep

Little Bo Peep

Little Bo Peep has lost her sheep
And can't tell where to find them.
Just leave them alone,
And they'll come home,
Wagging their tails behind them.

Little Bo Peep Accordion Book

Materials

- page 35, reproduced for each student
- 4 1/2″ x 18″ (11.5 x 45.5 cm) blue construction paper
- scissors
- glue

Steps to Follow

1. Guide students through the steps shown below to fold the accordion book.

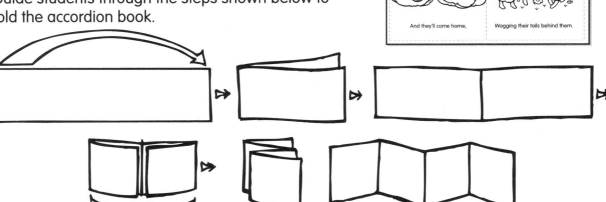

2. Students color and cut out the parts of the poem. They glue the parts in order, one to a page. When the glue is dry, fold the completed book.

3. Students recite the poem as they unfold their books to see the sheep follow Bo Peep. (The completed book can also stand up like a display board.)

Little Bo Peep

1. Color.

2. Cut.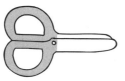

3. Paste.

Little Bo Peep

Name _____

Little Bo Peep has lost her sheep
And can't tell where to find them.

Just leave them alone,

And they'll come home,

Wagging their tails behind them.

=== EMC 2700 • © Evan-Moor Corp.

Materials

- 5″ x 7″ (13 x 18 cm) white construction paper
- page 37, reproduced for each student
- cotton balls
- paper fastener
- white and black crayons
- cotton swabs
- white glue

Steps to Follow

1. Cut the sheep's body out of white construction paper.

 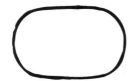

2. Use a cotton swab to place glue on the body. Lay cotton balls on the glued areas.

3. Using page 37, color the remaining parts black, cut them out, and glue together as shown. Add a small piece of cotton to the head for a topknot.

4. Attach the tail with a paper fastener so it can wag.

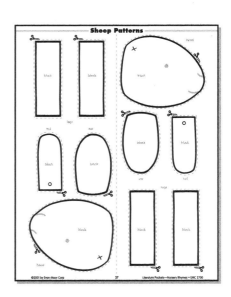

Sheep Patterns

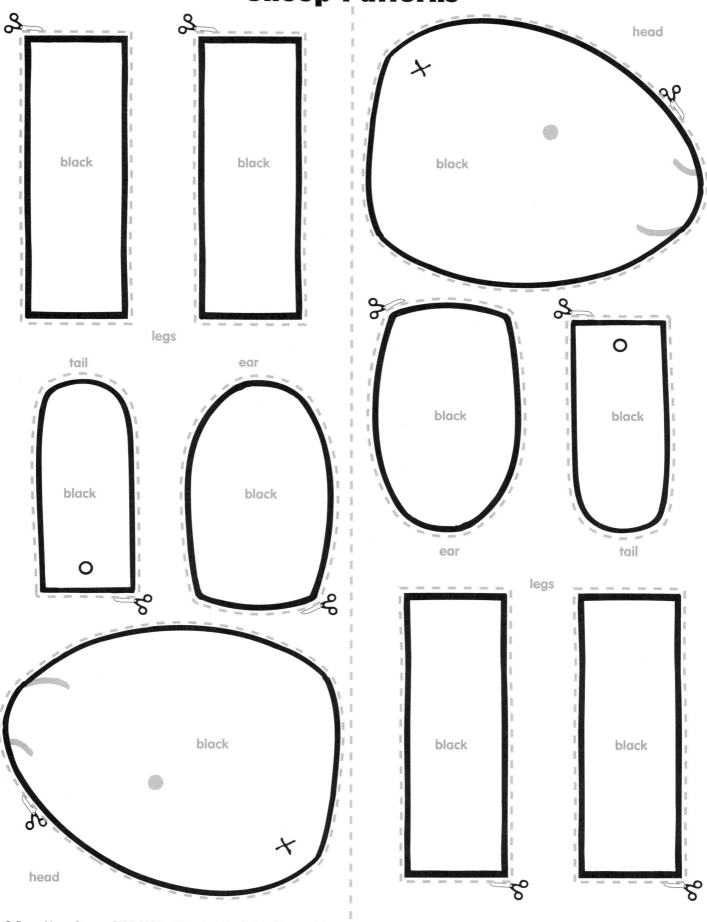

black

black

legs

head

black

tail

ear

black

black

black

ear

black

tail

legs

black

black

black

head

Name _____

Find Little Bo Peep's Lost Sheep

I found _____ sheep.

Literature Pockets—Nursery Rhymes • EMC 2700 • © Evan-Moor Corp.

Pocket 6
I Caught a Fish Alive!

Nursery Rhyme Chart
Follow the directions on page 1 for using the nursery rhyme chart.

Pop-up Fish Book
As students recite the rhyme, they open the cover of their little book and up pops a fish.

Ouch!
Will students remember their right hand after that hungry fish bites their little finger? This project is one more aid to help students remember the nursery rhyme.

I Caught It!
Students draw a picture and rewrite the rhyme to tell what they caught. Make copies of their work to bind in a cover for a class book. Put the originals in their I Caught a Fish Alive! pockets.

Pocket Label

I Caught a Fish Alive!

1, 2, 3, 4, 5,
I caught a fish alive.
6, 7, 8, 9, 10,
I let it go again.

Why did you let it go?
Because it bit my finger so.
Which finger did it bite?
The little one on the right.

Pop-up Fish Book

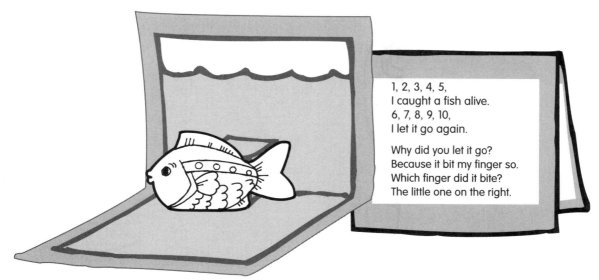

1, 2, 3, 4, 5,
I caught a fish alive.
6, 7, 8, 9, 10,
I let it go again.

Why did you let it go?
Because it bit my finger so.
Which finger did it bite?
The little one on the right.

Materials

- page 42, reproduced for each student
- 6″ x 9″ (15 x 23 cm) blue construction paper
- black marking pen

Steps to Follow

To make the pop-up form:

1. Cut out the pop-up form. Color the "water" blue.
2. Fold on the fold line. Cut on the cut lines.
3. Fold the tab down and crease it. Fold the tab back up.
4. Open the paper. Pull the tab through until the paper closes. Crease all folds.

To add the fish:

1. Color and cut out the fish.
2. Put glue on the pop-up tab and attach the fish.
3. Add "water" by drawing wavy lines.

To add the cover:

1. Fold the blue construction paper in half.
2. Close the pop-up page. Put glue on the back of one side. Lay it in the folder and press.
3. Flip the cover over. Open the cover and put glue on the other side of the pop-up page. Close the cover and press firmly.
4. Cut out the nursery rhyme and glue it to the front of the cover.

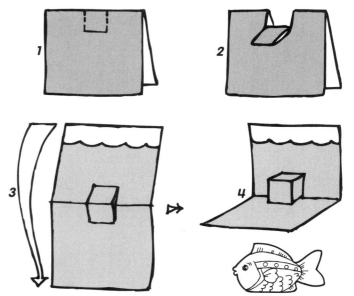

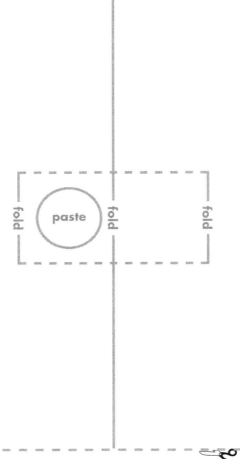

1, 2, 3, 4, 5,
I caught a fish alive.
6, 7, 8, 9, 10,
I let it go again.

Why did you let it go?
Because it bit my finger so.
Which finger did it bite?
The little one on the right.

Ouch!

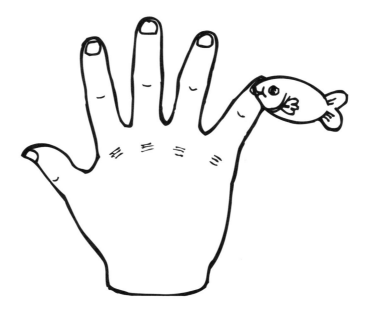

Materials
- 9″ x 12″ (23 x 30.5 cm) construction paper
- page 44, reproduced on construction paper (one fish per child)
- glue
- scissors
- crayons

Steps to Follow

1. Have students work in pairs to trace their right hands on construction paper. They can add details such as fingernails with crayons.

2. Provide each student with one fish from page 44. The fish should be cut out and glued to the little finger.

3. Students use the hand being bitten by the fish as they recite the nursery rhyme.

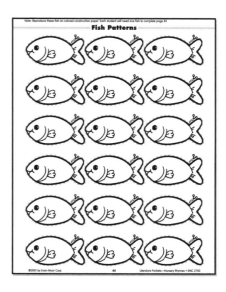

I Caught a Fish Alive!

Fish Patterns

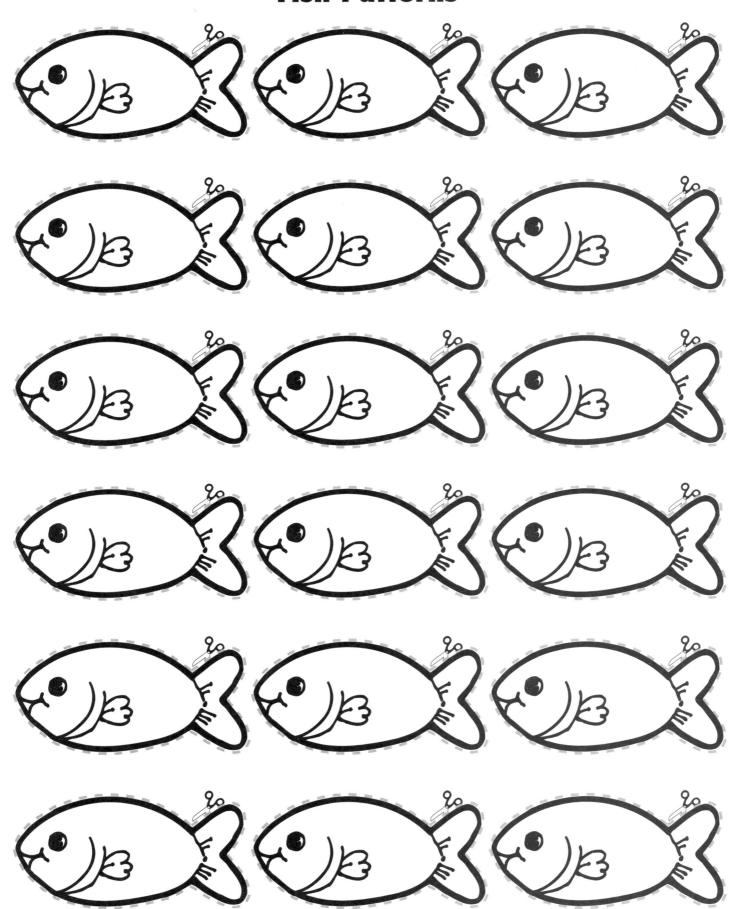

Note: Reproduce this page for students to use with "I Caught It!" on page 39.

Name _____

I Caught It!

1, 2, 3, 4, 5,

I caught a _____ alive.

6, 7, 8, 9, 10,

I let it go again.

Pocket 7
Pease Porridge

Nursery Rhyme Chart...
Follow the directions on page 1 for using the nursery rhyme chart.

Peas in a Pod..
Students slip the peas into the gigantic pod in order to practice sequencing as they recite the rhyme.

How Do You Like Your Pease Porridge? ....
Pease porridge is an old English food. Make pease porridge following the recipe on page 52 or use canned pea soup (leave it thicker than usual to be more "porridgy." Have a tasting party sharing pease porridge hot and pease porridge cold. Then create a class graph to answer the question, "Do you like your pease porridge hot or cold best?"

A Recipe—Pease Porridge...
Here is a simple recipe for pease porridge to send home in students' pockets.

I Like It Hot. I Like It Cold...
Students cut out the pot and glue a sentence to the front and another sentence to the back. They then draw or write things they like to eat hot on the "hot" side and things they like to eat cold on the "cold" side.

Pocket Label

Pease Porridge

Literature Pockets—Nursery Rhymes • EMC 2700 • © Evan-Moor Corp.

Pease Porridge

Pease porridge hot,
Pease porridge cold,
Pease porridge in the pot
Nine days old.

Some like it hot,
Some like it cold,
Some like it in the pot
Nine days old.

Peas in a Pod

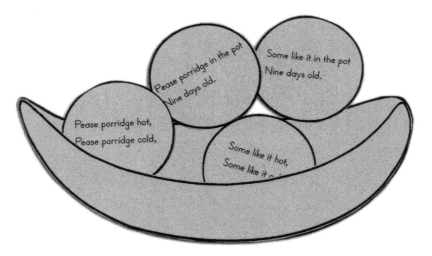

Materials
- pages 49 and 50, reproduced on green paper for each student
- glue
- scissors

Steps to Follow

1. Cut out the two parts of the pea pod. Put glue along the edge where indicated. Place the two pieces together and let the glue dry.

2. Cut out the peas. Slip them into the pod in the correct order.

3. Students pull out the peas as a reminder as they recite the rhyme.

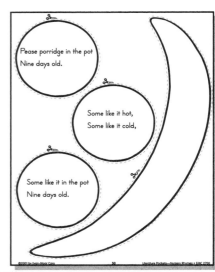

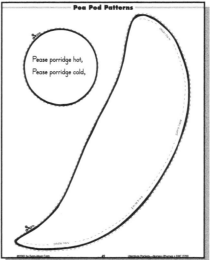

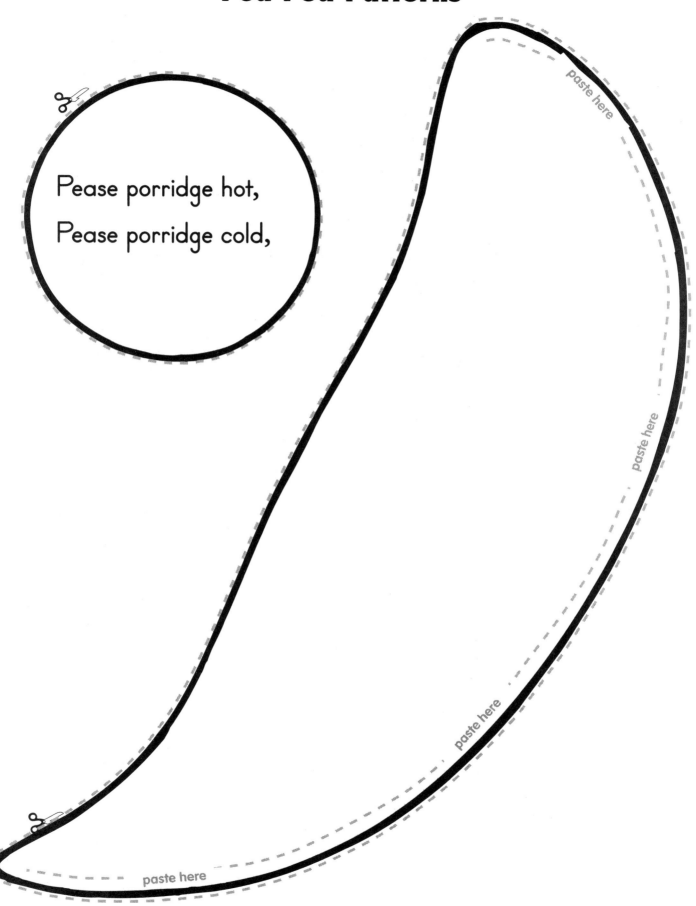

Pease porridge hot,

Pease porridge cold,

paste here

paste here

paste here

paste here

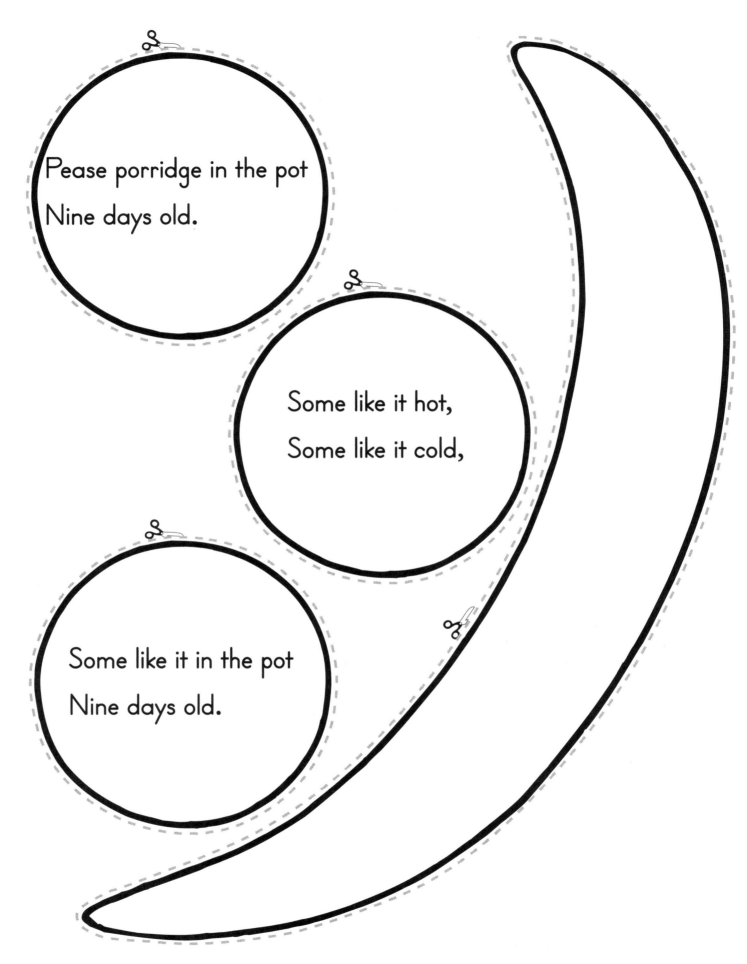

Pease porridge in the pot
Nine days old.

Some like it hot,
Some like it cold,

Some like it in the pot
Nine days old.

 Literature Pockets—Nursery Rhymes • EMC 2700 • © Evan-Moor Corp.

How Do You Like Your Pease Porridge?

Materials

- pease porridge (both hot and cold), using recipe on page 52 or canned pea soup
- small bowls and spoons
- recipe on page 52, reproduced for each child to take home
- chart paper
- black marking pen
- gray construction paper
- pot template below

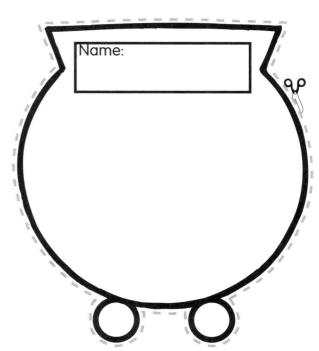

Steps to Follow

1. Prepare these in advance:
   a. pease porridge
   b. a chart labeled "I like it hot. I like it cold."
   c. small pots cut from gray construction paper

2. Have some pease porridge at a comfortable eating temperature and some cold. Give each student a small serving at each temperature to taste.

3. Give each student one of the gray "porridge pots." Each student writes his or her name on the pot and places it on the graph to indicate whether he or she liked it best hot or cold.

4. Use the information on the completed graph to determine which way most students preferred the porridge.

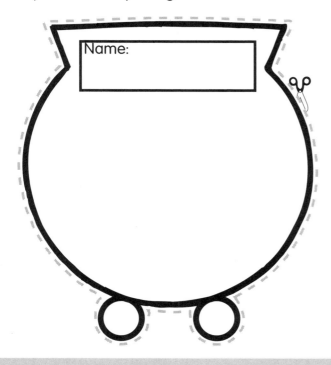

Pease Porridge

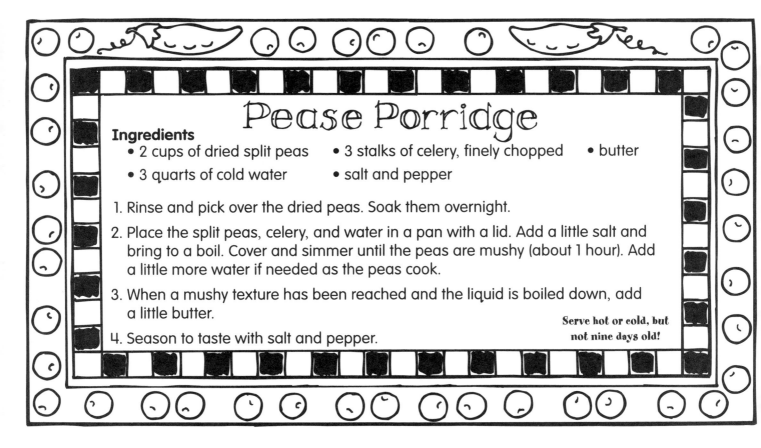

Pease Porridge

Ingredients
- 2 cups of dried split peas
- 3 quarts of cold water
- 3 stalks of celery, finely chopped
- salt and pepper
- butter

1. Rinse and pick over the dried peas. Soak them overnight.

2. Place the split peas, celery, and water in a pan with a lid. Add a little salt and bring to a boil. Cover and simmer until the peas are mushy (about 1 hour). Add a little more water if needed as the peas cook.

3. When a mushy texture has been reached and the liquid is boiled down, add a little butter.

4. Season to taste with salt and pepper.

Serve hot or cold, but not nine days old!

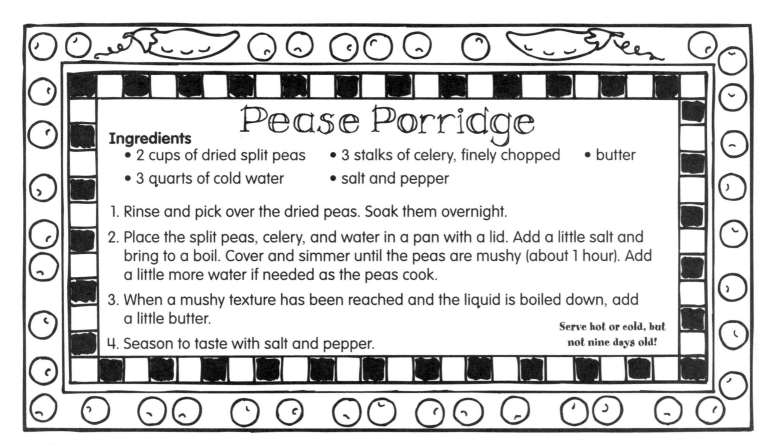

Pease Porridge

Ingredients
- 2 cups of dried split peas
- 3 quarts of cold water
- 3 stalks of celery, finely chopped
- salt and pepper
- butter

1. Rinse and pick over the dried peas. Soak them overnight.

2. Place the split peas, celery, and water in a pan with a lid. Add a little salt and bring to a boil. Cover and simmer until the peas are mushy (about 1 hour). Add a little more water if needed as the peas cook.

3. When a mushy texture has been reached and the liquid is boiled down, add a little butter.

4. Season to taste with salt and pepper.

Serve hot or cold, but not nine days old!

I Like It Hot. I Like It Cold.

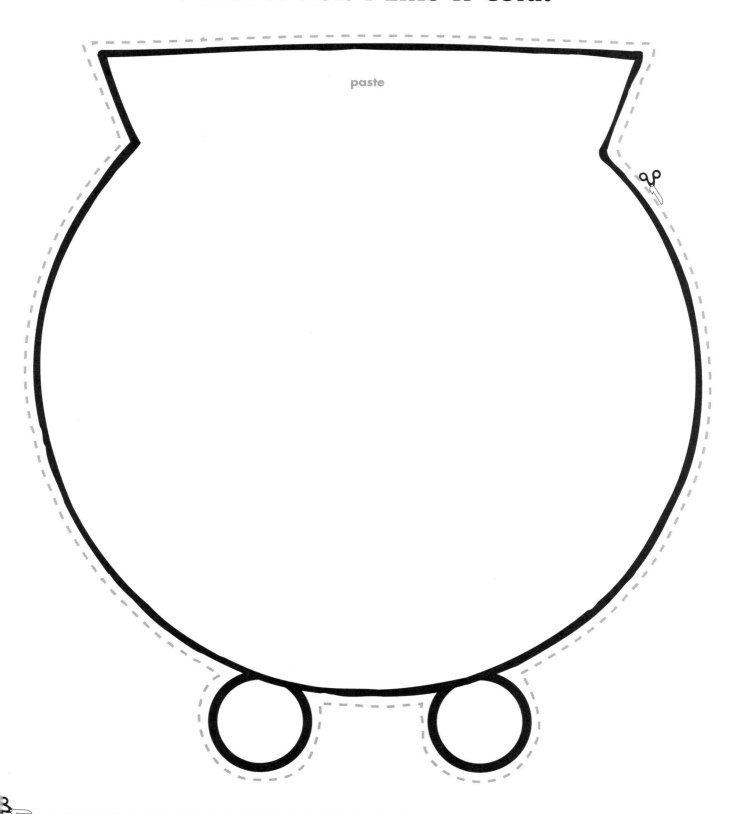

paste

I like to eat these things **hot.** I like to eat these things **cold.**

Nursery Rhyme Chart ....page 55
Follow the directions on page 1 for using the nursery rhyme chart.

A Tiny Book ....page 56
Cut the pages apart and then put them in order. Punch holes in the left side (an adult may need to do this) and tie the pages together with a piece of string. Read the book together and then put it in students' Rub-a-Dub-Dub pockets.

Finger Puppets ....pages 57 and 58
Students use these delightful finger puppets as they recite the nursery rhyme to dramatize the three men sailing in their tub.

Three _____ in a Tub..............................pages 59 and 60
In this activity, students decide for themselves who is sailing in the tub. They rewrite the verse, draw new characters, and then take them for a rousing ride upon the waves.

Pocket Label

Rub-a-Dub-Dub

Rub-a-dub-dub
Three men in a tub,
And who do you think they be?
The butcher, the baker,
The candlestick maker,
And they all set out to sea.

Color. Cut apart. Punch holes. Tie.

Rub-a-Dub-Dub

Name _____

Rub-a-dub-dub
Three men in a tub,
And who do you think they be?

The butcher,

The baker,

The candlestick maker,

And they all set out to sea.

Finger Puppets

Materials
- page 58, reproduced for each student
- crayons
- glue
- scissors

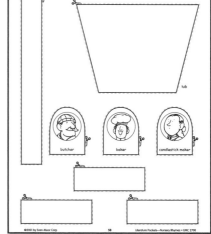

Steps to Follow
1. Color and cut out the puppet pieces.

2. Glue the paper strips as shown to make "rings."

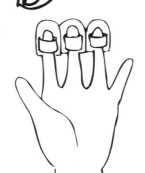

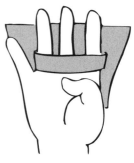
glue

3. Glue the butcher, baker, and candlestick maker to the small rings. Glue the tub to the large ring.

4. Place the tub over one hand and the remaining puppets on the fingers of the other hand. Hold the tub puppet in front of the finger puppets while reciting the rhyme.

Finger Puppet Patterns

Rub-a-Dub-Dub

tub

butcher

baker

candlestick maker

Materials

- page 60, reproduced for each student
- 9″ x 12″ (23 x 30.5 cm) blue construction paper
- plastic straw
- crayons
- glue
- scissors

Steps to Follow

1. Cut waves along the bottom of the blue paper and fold it up about one-fourth of the page. Open it back up and make a short slit along the center of the fold. (An adult will need to do this.) Put glue along the side edges and fold the "waves" back up.

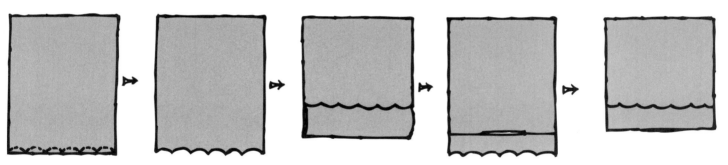

2. Complete the sentence strip by writing in the type of character that will be in the boat. Glue the strip onto the water.

> Rub-a-dub-dub
> Three _____ in a tub.

3. Students decide what three characters (people, animals, or imaginary creatures) are going to ride in the tub. They draw their three characters in the circles on the tub.

4. Cut out the picture and tape it to the top half of the straw. Slip the straw through the slit in the bottom of the paper. By wiggling the straw, students can make it look like the tub is sailing on the water.

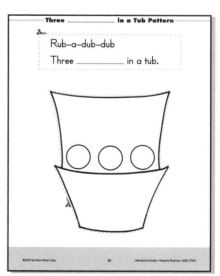

Rub-a-Dub-Dub

Rub-a-dub-dub

Three _____ in a tub.

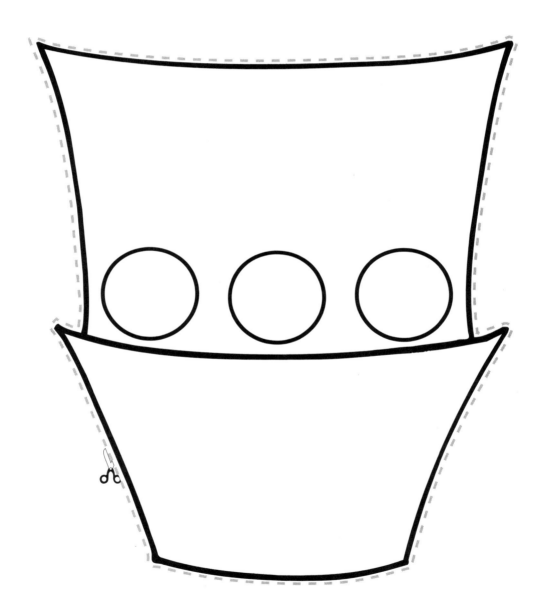

Pocket 9
Sing a Song of Sixpence

Follow the directions on page 1 for using the nursery rhyme chart.

Make a gigantic pie with a top that unfolds to reveal the blackbirds made by students. Lift the top of the pie as students recite the verses of "Sing a Song of Sixpence." They then make pies of their own to go into their pockets.

Students paste characters from the nursery rhyme in the correct location as they recall what occurs in the rhyme. Then they staple the pages together into a little booklet to read and place in their Sing a Song of Sixpence pockets.

Pocket Label

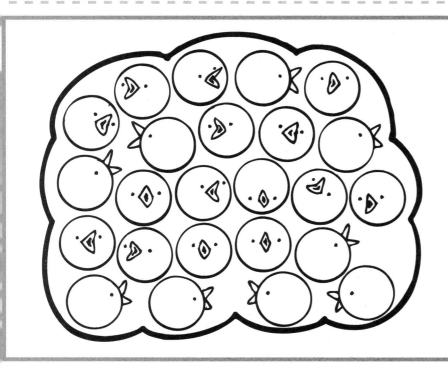

Sing a Song of Sixpence

Sing a Song of Sixpence

Sing a song of sixpence,
A pocket full of rye;
Four and twenty blackbirds
Baked in a pie.

When the pie was opened,
The birds began to sing;
Wasn't that a dainty dish
To set before the king?

The king was in his counting house,
Counting out his money.
The queen was in the parlor,
Eating bread and honey.

The maid was in the garden,
Hanging out the clothes;
When down came a blackbird
And snapped off her nose!

Four and Twenty Blackbirds Baked in a Pie
Class Pie

Materials
- two 20″ x 28″ (51 x 71 cm) pieces of brown butcher paper
- page 64, reproduced for each student
- crayons
- black marking pen
- scissors

Steps to Follow

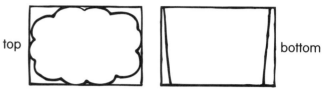

1. Sketch the pie shell top and bottom onto the two pieces of brown butcher paper.

2. Cut out the pie. Staple the bottom to a bulletin board.

3. Add details to the top with a black marking pen. Make a crease in the top as shown. Staple the top to the bulletin board, leaving the bottom edge open so it can be lifted to show the blackbirds inside.

4. Students color and cut out blackbirds until there are 24. Pin the blackbirds under the pie top. (When you are ready to take down the pie, students place their blackbirds in their Sing a Song of Sixpence pockets.)

5. Recite the first verse of the nursery rhyme, lifting the lid to see 4 and 20 blackbirds "baked" in the pie. Variation—Change the number of blackbirds each day for counting practice.

Students' Pies

Materials
- pages 64 and 65, reproduced for each student
- crayons
- scissors
- glue

Steps to Follow

1. Color and cut out the pie form.

2. Fold on the fold lines.

3. Cut out the poem and glue it to the bottom of the pie.

4. Color and cut out the blackbirds and glue them inside the pie.

Sing a song of sixpence,
A pocket full of rye;
Four and twenty blackbirds
Baked in a pie.

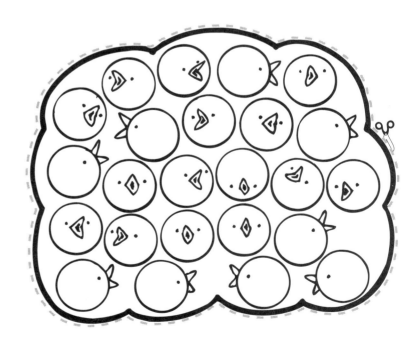

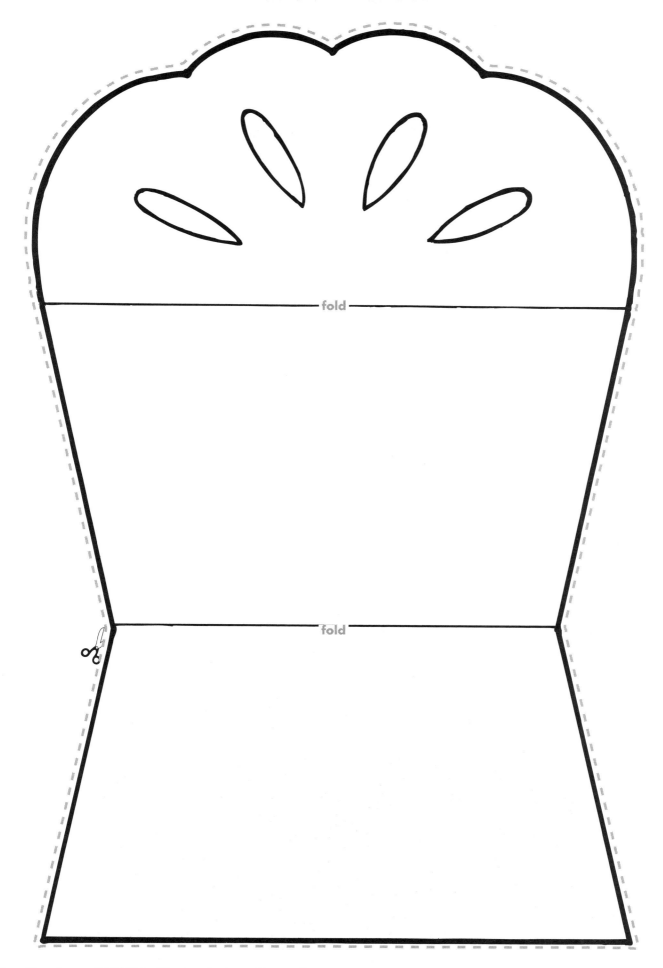

fold

fold

Materials

- pages 67 and 68, reproduced for each student
- scissors
- glue
- crayons
- stapler

Steps to Follow

1. Color all pieces.
2. Cut out the king, queen, maid, blackbirds, and crow.
3. Glue each character in the correct setting.
4. Cut out each completed picture.
5. Put the pages in order and staple them together.

Sing a song of sixpence, A pocket full of rye;

name

Four and twenty blackbirds
Baked in a pie.
When the pie was opened
The birds began to sing.
Wasn't that a dainty dish
To set before the king?

paste

The king was in his
counting house,
Counting out his money.

paste

The queen was in the parlor,
Eating bread and honey.

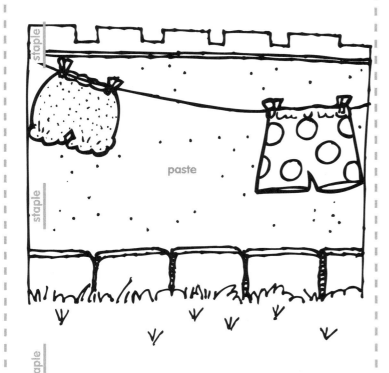

The maid was in the garden,
Hanging out the clothes;

When down came a blackbird
And snapped off her nose!

Nursery Rhyme Chart... page 70
Follow the directions on page 1 for using the nursery rhyme chart.

Pig Puppet...**pages 71 and 72**
This amusing mitt puppet fits over students' hands for a lively recitation of the nursery rhyme.

A True Book of Pigs...**pages 73 and 74**
Cut the pages apart and staple them in order to make a little book filled with interesting facts about pigs and hogs. Read and discuss the book together and then place in students' pockets.

To Market, To Market... page 75
As a class, create a list of couplets about things students might buy at the market. Write these on a chart. Each student selects one "purchase" to copy and illustrate.

What Is a Bun?.. page 76
Read the information given on the page together to find out what a bun could be. Students then circle all of the buns they find on the page.

Pocket Label

To Market, To Market

To Market, To Market

To market, to market, to buy a fat pig,
Home again, home again, jiggety jig.

To market, to market, to buy a fat hog,
Home again, home again, jiggety jog.

To market, to market, to buy a plum bun,
Home again, home again, market is done.

Pig Puppet

Materials

- 9″ x 12″ (23 x 30.5 cm) pink construction paper
- page 72, reproduced on pink construction paper
- piece of foam packing for spacer
- pipe cleaner piece for tail
- glue
- cellophane tape
- black crayon or marking pen

Steps to Follow

1. Follow these steps to make the basic mitt for the puppet.

2. Cut out the ears and paste them to the back of the mitt. Fold the ears down toward the front of the puppet.

3. Cut out the snout. Add black nostrils. Glue a foam packing piece in the center of the puppet for a spacer. Glue the snout to the foam piece.

4. Add black eyes and a mouth.

5. Curl the pipe cleaner for the tail. Tape the tail to the back of the puppet.

6. Glue the nursery rhyme to the back of the puppet.

7. Slip the puppet on a hand and recite the rhyme for a friend.

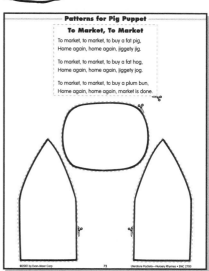

Patterns for Pig Puppet
To Market, To Market

To market, to market, to buy a fat pig,
Home again, home again, jiggety jig.

To market, to market, to buy a fat hog,
Home again, home again, jiggety jog.

To market, to market, to buy a plum bun,
Home again, home again, market is done.

©2001 by Evan-Moor Corp. 73 Literature Pockets—Nursery Rhymes • EMC 2700

Patterns for Pig Puppet

To Market, To Market

To market, to market, to buy a fat pig,
Home again, home again, jiggety jig.

To market, to market, to buy a fat hog,
Home again, home again, jiggety jog.

To market, to market, to buy a plum bun,
Home again, home again, market is done.

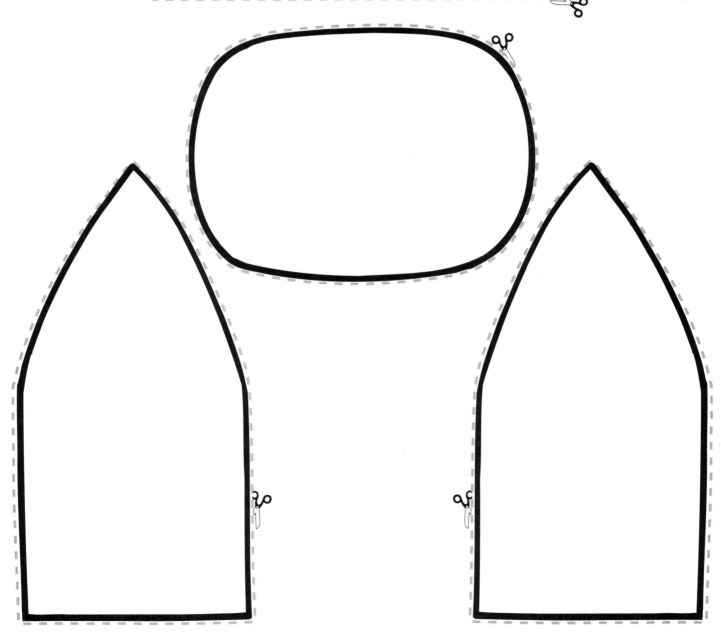

A True Book of Pigs

Name _____

This is a pig family.
Father is a boar.
Mother is a sow.
The babies are piglets.

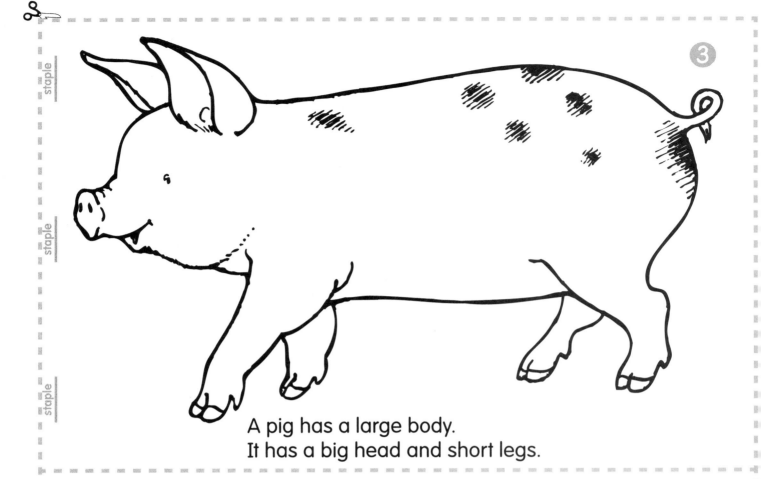

A pig has a large body.
It has a big head and short legs.

A pig's nose is called a snout.
A pig can use its snout to dig food out of the ground.

Name _____

To Market, To Market

To market, to market, to buy a _____.

Home again, home again, _____.

What Is a Bun?

Name _____

A bun is a kind of bread roll. It can be plain.
It can be sweet. It can have spices and dried fruit in it.
A plum bun is a sweet bun with dried plums.

Circle the buns.

Nursery Rhyme Chart.................................**page 78**
Follow the directions on page 1 for using the nursery rhyme chart.

One, Two, Buckle My Shoe........................**pages 79 and 80**
Follow the directions to make a layer book showing each couplet of the poem.

Magic Counting String ....**page 81**
Students use a "magic string" to form each number from the rhyme.

What Goes Together?................................**pages 82 and 83**
Students cut and paste the numbers and number words beside each set of objects. They then paste the two pages together at the paste line to make one long strip.

Rhyming Puzzle................................**pages 84–86**
Students practice finding rhyming words using these three-part puzzles.

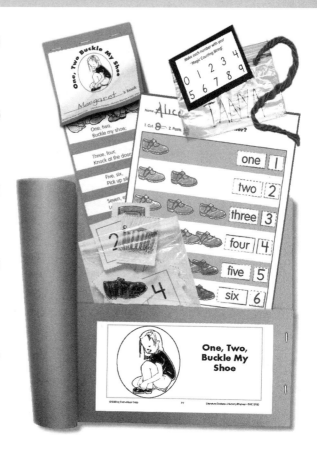

Pocket Label

One, Two, Buckle My Shoe

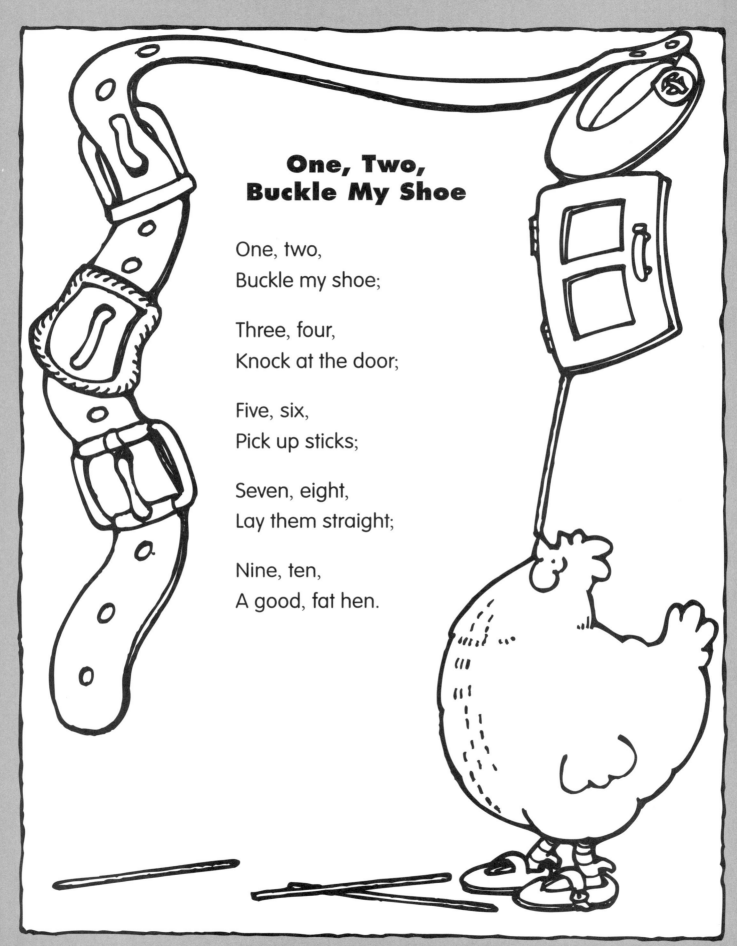

One, Two,
Buckle My Shoe

One, two,
Buckle my shoe;

Three, four,
Knock at the door;

Five, six,
Pick up sticks;

Seven, eight,
Lay them straight;

Nine, ten,
A good, fat hen.

Literature Pockets—Nursery Rhymes • EMC 2700 • © Evan-Moor Corp.

One, Two, Buckle My Shoe

Use this bookmaking activity to review the couplets of the nursery rhyme.

Materials

- construction paper for book pages (pages may be all one color or assorted colors)
  - 4″ x 4″ (10 x 10 cm)
  - 4″ x 5″ (10 x 13 cm)
  - 4″ x 6″ (10 x 15 cm)
  - 4″ x 7″ (10 x 18 cm)
  - 4″ x 8″ (10 x 20 cm)
  - 4″ x 9″ (10 x 23 cm)
- page 80, reproduced for each student
- crayons, marking pens, or colored pencils
- scissors
- glue
- stapler

Steps to Follow

1. Place the pieces of paper in order as shown. Staple along the top edge through all pages. (An adult may need to do this.)

2. Read each of the couplets on page 80. Color and cut out the sections. Glue them in order on the pages of the book. Align the bottom edge of each couplet with the bottom edge of each page.

3. Lift each flap of the book to see the illustration of the couplet as it is read.

One, Two, Buckle My Shoe

_____'s book

One, two,
Buckle my shoe;

Three, four,
Knock at the door;

Five, six,
Pick up sticks;

Seven, eight,
Lay them straight;

Nine, ten,
A good, fat hen.

Magic Counting String

Materials
- self-locking plastic bag for each student
- 12″ (30.5 cm) piece of sturdy twine or yarn for each student
- card at the bottom of this page, reproduced for each student
- 3″ x 5″ (7.5 x 13 cm) colored construction paper for each student
- permanent marking pen
- scissors
- glue

Steps to Follow
1. Glue a copy of the card to a piece of construction paper.
2. Place the card and piece of twine in a plastic bag.
3. Write the student's name on the plastic bag with permanent marking pen.
4. Students take the twine out of the plastic bag to practice forming the numbers from 0 to 9.

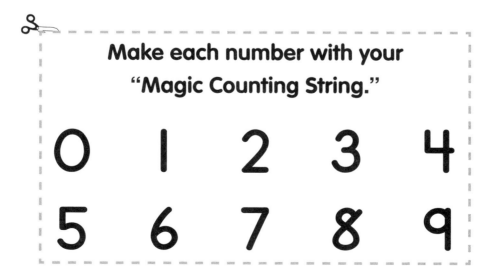

Make each number with your
"Magic Counting String."

0 1 2 3 4
5 6 7 8 9

Name _____

What Goes Together?

1. Cut. 2. Paste.

paste

paste

paste

paste

paste

paste

paste

paste

paste

paste

paste

paste

paste

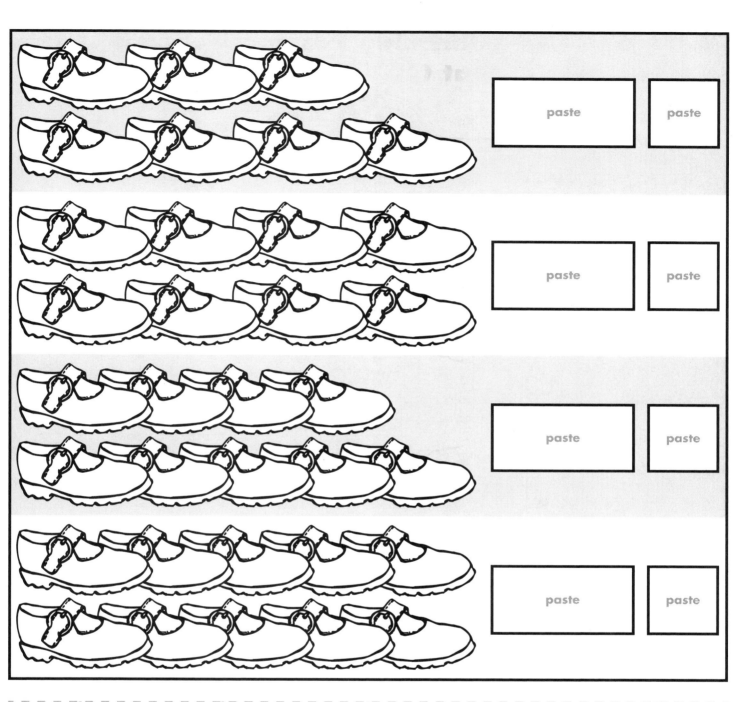

2 9 4 7 1 10 6 3 8 5

three five two one four

ten seven nine eight six

Rhyming Puzzle

Materials

- pages 85 and 86, reproduced on white construction paper for each student
- scissors
- glue
- self-locking plastic bag

Steps to Follow

1. Students cut out all of the puzzle pieces.

2. They name each number and then find two pictures that rhyme with it.

3. Store the puzzle pieces in a plastic bag between uses.

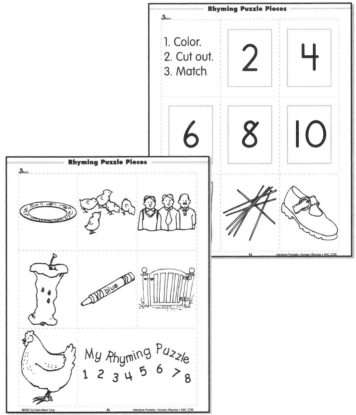

Rhyming Puzzle Pieces

1. Color.

2. Cut.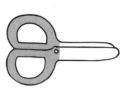

3. Match.

2

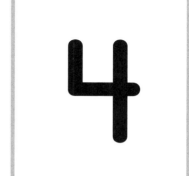

4

6

8

10

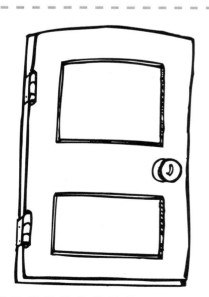

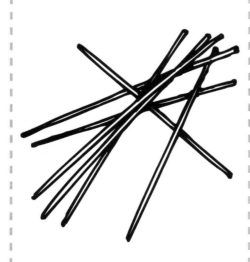

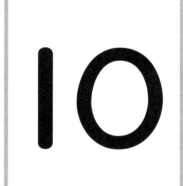

My Rhyming Puzzle
1 2 3 4 5 6 7 8

Pocket 12
Diddle, Diddle, Dumpling

Nursery Rhyme Chart ....**page 88**
Follow the directions on page 1 for using the nursery rhyme chart.

Socks Off or Socks On? ....**pages 89 and 90**
Using feet patterns, students help create a graph to show whether they go to bed with their socks off or on.

Time for Bed, John ....**pages 91–93**
Students create a bed for John and then lift the blanket to tuck John in for a good night's sleep as they recite the rhyme. John's blanket contains the words to the nursery rhyme.

Sort the Socks..............................**page 94**
Students cut and paste to match the two socks that make a pair. When the page is complete, have students explain what "clues" they used to make their matches.

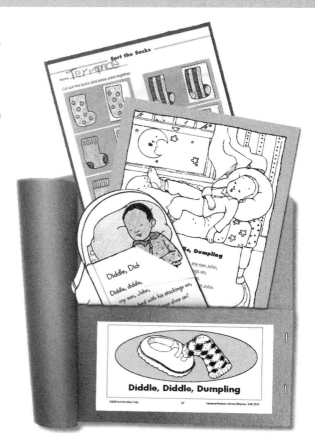

Pocket Label

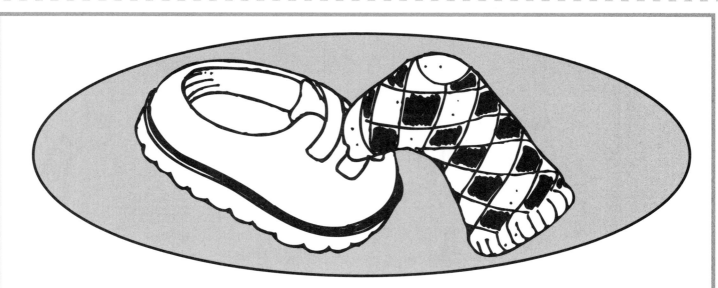

Diddle, Diddle, Dumpling

Diddle, Diddle, Dumpling

Diddle, diddle, dumpling, my son John,
Went to bed with his stockings on;
One shoe off and one shoe on,
Diddle, diddle, dumpling, my son John.

Socks Off or Socks On?

Create a graph to show students' answers to the question, "Do you sleep with your socks off or on?"

Materials

- page 90, reproduced to provide two feet for each student
- large sheet of chart paper
- black marking pen
- scissors
- glue

Steps to Follow

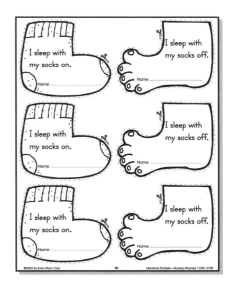

1. Prepare a pictograph form by marking the chart paper as shown above.

2. Ask students to select two bare feet if they sleep with their socks off or two socks if they sleep with their socks on. They write their names on each of the feet. One foot is glued to the correct column on the graph. The second foot goes in the students' Diddle, Diddle, Dumpling pockets.

3. Follow up by asking questions about the graph.
   How many children sleep in socks?
   How many children sleep with bare feet?
   Do more children sleep in socks or with bare feet?

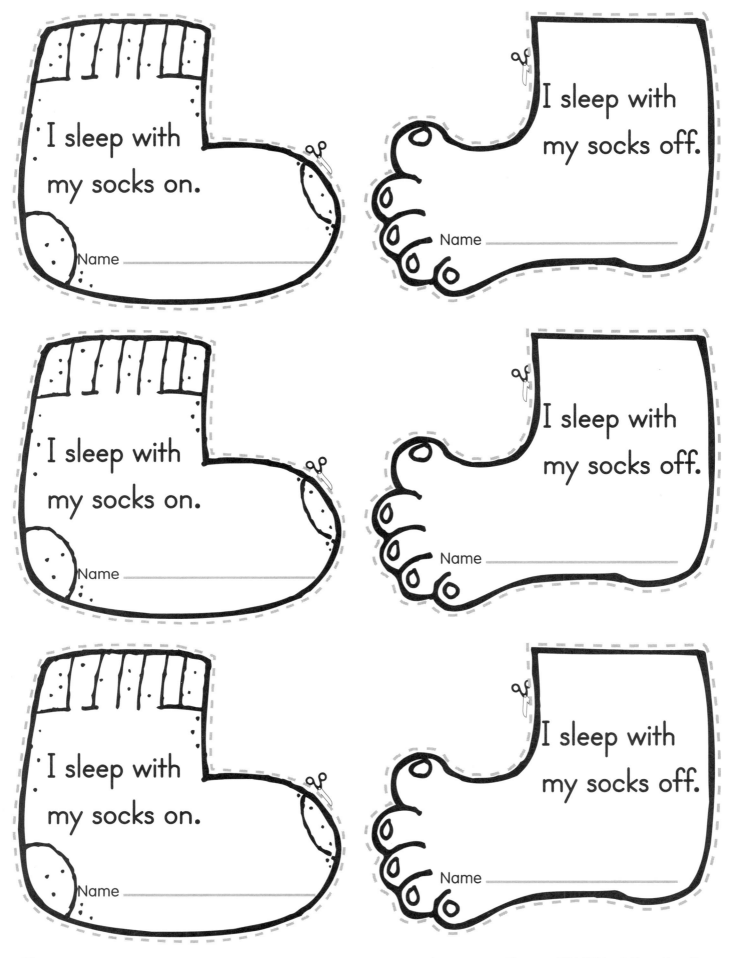

I sleep with my socks on.

Name _____

I sleep with my socks off.

Name _____

I sleep with my socks on.

Name _____

I sleep with my socks off.

Name _____

I sleep with my socks on.

Name _____

I sleep with my socks off.

Name _____

Time for Bed, John

Diddle, Diddle, Dumpling

Diddle, diddle, dumpling,
  my son John,
Went to bed with his stockings on;
One shoe off and one shoe on,
Diddle, diddle, dumpling,
  my son John.

Materials
- pages 92 and 93, reproduced for each student
- scissors
- glue

Steps to Follow
1. Color and cut out the bed.

2. Color and cut out the blanket. Put glue along the marked edge. Glue the blanket to the bed. After the glue dries, fold the blanket back and forth a few times to make it easy to lift when John is put to bed.

3. Color John's pajamas, shoe, and socks. Cut out John. Lift the blanket and tuck him into bed.

4. Students recite the verse, and then lift the blanket to see John's feet with "one shoe off and one shoe on."

Variation
Students trace around the pattern for John, and then draw in their own faces and the clothes they wear to bed.

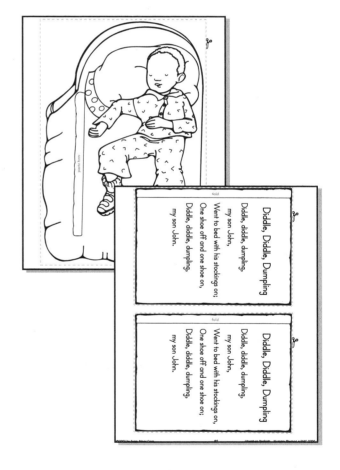

Diddle, Diddle, Dumpling

paste here

fold

Diddle, Diddle, Dumpling

Diddle, diddle, dumpling,
   my son John,
Went to bed with his stockings on;
One shoe off and one shoe on,
Diddle, diddle, dumpling,
   my son John.

fold

Diddle, Diddle, Dumpling

Diddle, diddle, dumpling,
   my son John,
Went to bed with his stockings on,
One shoe off and one shoe on;
Diddle, diddle, dumpling,
   my son John.

Sort the Socks

Cut out the socks and paste pairs together.

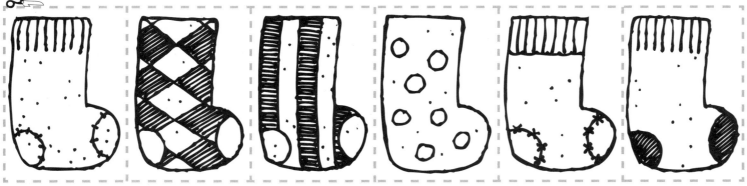

Literature Pockets—Nursery Rhymes • EMC 2700 • © Evan-Moor Corp.

Nursery Rhyme Cubes

Materials
- two 1-quart milk cartons
- page 96, reproduced for each student
- crayons or colored pencils
- permanent marking pen
- cellophane tape
- scissors
- glue

Steps to Follow
1. Wash the milk cartons and dry thoroughly.

2. Measure up 3″ (7.5 cm) from the bottom of the container. Draw a line around the container with a permanent marking pen. Cut off the measured amount of the container.

3. Slip two bottoms together to make a cube. Tape the sides together.

4. Color, cut out, and glue one picture to each side of the cube. (There is a picture for each nursery rhyme in this book. Select the rhymes your students have learned. If they know all 12 rhymes, make two cubes.)

How to Use
A student rolls one cube, looks at the picture on the side that lands faceup, and either names the rhyme or recites it. If more than one student is using the cube, pass it around, with each student taking a turn.

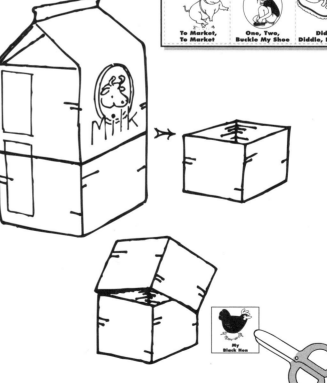

**A Little
Bird**

**Little
Miss Muffet**

**My
Black Hen**

**Jack
and Jill**

**Little
Bo Peep**

**I Caught a
Fish Alive!**

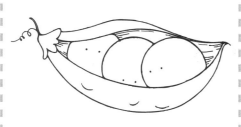

**Pease
Porridge**

**Rub-a-
Dub-Dub**

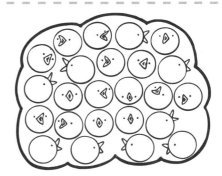

**Sing a Song
of Sixpence**

**To Market,
To Market**

**One, Two,
Buckle My Shoe**

**Diddle,
Diddle, Dumpling**

Literature Pockets—Nursery Rhymes • EMC 2700 • © Evan-Moor Corp.